Tabernacle Prayer
Frequencies of Power

Cleansed, Refined and Accepted

Fit to Fight in the "Spirit of Torah"

Shir le

Unless otherwise indicated, Scripture quotations are taken from the NEW AMERICAN STANDARD BIBLE, (NASB). Copyright 1960, 1962, 1963, 1968, 1971, 1972, 1973, 1975, 1977, 1995, by The Lockman Foundation. Used by permission. All rights reserved.

Changes made by the author include: "The LORD" used in NASB scripture quotations has been replaced with the Hebrew tetragrammaton **YHVH** and "Jesus" has been replaced with **Yashua**.

Copyright © All rights reserved. 2015

Tabernacle Prayer Frequencies of Power
Cleansed, Refined and Accepted
Fit to Fight in the "Spirit of Torah"
by Shir le

Printed in the United States of America

ISBN-13: 978-1517015091
ISBN-10:151701509X

Dedication

To the Giver and Sustainer of ALL life

YHVH Yashua --- without whom we have no life!

Table of Contents

Introduction…..............................11

A Word from Steve…................15

Entering In…..............................26

The Brazen Altar…....................40

The Laver….................................58

The Menorah…..........................68

The Table of Showbread….......84

The Incense Altar…...................92

The Ark of the Covenant….......99

ACKNOWLEDGMENTS

This is a work of the Ruach haKodesh, also known as the Holy Spirit. I am only the vessel He chose to use to put these words and understandings to paper; I take full responsibility for any errors and/or misrepresentations of His words.

Steve and I pray that YHVH Yashua meet with you, teach you, refine you, and embrace you along your journey!

Introduction

This book serves the purpose as guide to help facilitate your journey to the Throne of the Great I AM. Our coming into the presence of YHVH, Creator of All, must be with humility, reverence, great awe and respect for the King of Kings and Adonai ha Adonim!

The prophets of Baal in the confrontation on Mount Carmel were calling on the name of Baal from morning until noon saying, "O Baal, answer us." But there was no voice and no one answered. And they leaped about the altar which they made.

It came about at noon, that Elijah mocked them and said, "Call out with a loud voice, for he is a god; either he is occupied or gone aside, or is on a journey, or perhaps he is asleep and needs to be awakened."

So they cried with a loud voice and cut themselves according to their custom with swords and lances until the blood gushed out on them.

When midday was past, they raved until the time of the offering of the *evening* sacrifice; but there was no voice, no one answered, and no one paid attention. (1Kings 18:26-29)

This is how those who think YHVH is their fairy godmother or a great cosmic vending machine act; they expect their god to respond with his hand when they call. The Great and Almighty YHVH hears us when we call out to Him according to 2Chronicles 7:14, and My people who are called by My name [when they] humble themselves and pray and seek My face and turn from their wicked ways, then I will hear from heaven, [and] will forgive their sin...

Tabernacle Prayer is about choices; making a choice to enter in through the gateway veil; to submit to YHVH's cleansing and character refinement so that we may be able to stand as the pure, spotless Bride of Yashua haMashiach.

Please refrain from thinking you have to go through this journey all at once. Spend as much time at each article of furniture as you need too. There are scriptures included for your meditation; and prayers for your reflection. Ask the Ruach haKodesh/Holy Spirit to bring to your mind things or people that you may need to seek forgiveness for; make restitution to; or repent of. Be quick to acknowledge your guilt and seek YHVH's mercy as you repent for your wrong and/or lack of doing. The accuser of the brethren is before the throne accusing us day and night, and with good cause --- we are guilty! But let us not forget that our Intercessor Yashua is also before the throne ready with His blood to cover us and silence the accuser of the brethren if we will only come to Him in repentance and humility [for] if we confess our sins, He is faithful and righteous to forgive us our sins and to cleanse us from all unrighteousness. (1John 1:9)

You will find references to contemporary worship songs that may be helpful to you to look up on the internet (we suggest youtube.com) to aid your worship experience in addition to the Tabernacle Prayer CD which is an hour of harp music that begins with the lowest frequency, 396hz associated with the Brazen Altar and proceeds through all the articles of furniture to the highest frequency 852hz associated with the Ark of the Covenant. Each frequency has associated mental, emotional and relational benefits and combined with the suggested scripture and prayer meditations results in a very rich and fulfilling worship experience.

The subject of the Tabernacle is a vast wonderland, full of beauty, mystery and surprises of great love, mercy and displays of YHVH's unlimited compassion for His creation. To say that this small work encompasses the whole range of thought on this subject would be foolish indeed! Please keep in mind that this attempt at offering an experience of entering into the realm of the greatness of YHVH's love for His creation is just one, tiny facet of a glorious multi-faceted diamond.

The harp music CD companion to this book is from the Hebrew Scriptures as discovered through the guidance of the Ruach haKodesh by Steve Rees. To order the companion *Tabernacle Prayer* harp CD please contact us at either:

www.calmingharp.com   www.harpandstory.com

A Word from Steve

Introducing the spiritual exercise of prayer through the Wilderness Tabernacle of Moses it would be good to have an understanding of where the idea came from. The six Solfeggio frequencies as discovered in the 7th chapter of the Biblical book of Numbers --- 396 Hz, 417 Hz, 528 Hz, 639 Hz, 741 Hz, and 852 Hz, have a correlation to the six articles of furniture YHVH instructed Moses to build for the Tabernacle.

We are quick to add the understanding that we are not going "new age" with this information although the "new age" crowd has picked up on using these frequencies. We must remember that YHVH/God created these frequencies. The enemy does not create nor is he original – he only copies and usually puts a twist into the scheme at the same time. Truth with a twist becomes a lie or at least a distortion to get us sidetracked from the plans and purposes of our Heavenly Abba. We believe that it is important to discover YHVH's original design and purpose and restore that understanding so that we can benefit from what He has created for us and gain its full benefits.

If you think about it, the enemy always tries to take our focus away from YHVH and place the focus on ourselves or the enemy or things. If it is true, and I believe that it is, that YHVH gave us these frequencies to enhance our worship of and focus on Him, wouldn't it make sense that the enemy would try to pervert them so that they no longer served the purpose for which YHH intended them?

This seems to be exactly what the enemy has done. The new age crowd have taken these frequencies and used them to focus on the chakras in an effort to enhance individual performance. The focus is on self, helping a person to perform better, using these frequencies to "tune up" the body and its functioning. The focus has been turned away from the Creator to the created.

Even the work of Dr. Masaru Emoto on the effects of 528 Hz frequency on the freezing crystal patterns of water have been largely relegated into a focus on the natural phenomena of the frequency instead of bringing us into a greater understanding of how our Creator has provided a way through the frequencies to come back into phase with Him and restore our original patterns that He created us with. Considering that we are at least 75%

water, it is very important to understand that these frequencies actually do contribute in restoring us back into our original created design for health and wellness.

Not only are the frequencies powerful in this restoration, but the words used with these frequencies as well. Dr. Emoto also experimented with how words effect the crystal formation of frozen water and determined that they as well had profound effects. With that understanding, Shirley and I recorded the "Shalom Power Clips" CD that combined the frequencies of the Tabernacle with the words of YHVH found throughout scripture. As we learn to use these frequencies and the words of our Savior found in scripture, we have a powerful weapon with which to combat the enemy. Remember our weapons are not carnal but are powerful to the tearing down of strongholds. Resist the enemy and he will flee from you – Draw near to YHVH and He will draw near to you. I believe these frequencies are part of drawing near to our Heavenly Father.

Our Creator not only created us, but provided us with a way of being restored, both physically and spiritually. I find it fascinating that this information is being released into the body of Messiah at such a time in earth's history as we find ourselves. As the enemy has succeeded in destroying so much of YHVH's creation, Yahovah is releasing the knowledge and wisdom necessary to help restore what the enemy has tried to destroy. Amazing Grace!

In 2006, after listening to a presentation on the Song of the Lamb and the 144,000 I began asking myself, "What did the Psalms of David sound like"? Since I play the harp as did David, it seemed like a natural question. As a nurse I would take my harp into the hospital and play for my patients. I observed amazing effects on the physiology of sick people and saw how it appeared to be much the same as what we read about in the book of 1 Samuel when David played his harp, the troubling spirit or sickness left Saul.

In noting how the Hebrew language is very unique in that there is a meaning to every letter of the aleph-bet, and every letter has an associated number, it seemed that there might be a note or frequency that corresponded to each letter as well. In studying further, there was some information on Cymatics that gave a positive witness to this idea. Hebrew letters spoken into a microphone and sounded out on a sand plate actually formed the shape of some of the Hebrew letters in the sand. In my mind this verified that there was a connection between the physical letter and sound.

Another understanding came from the work of Joseph Puleo in working with the Hebrew text of Numbers chapter 7 and applying an ancient mathematical system

called the Pythagorean Skene to determine the solfeggio frequencies that we previously mentioned. Another witness to these frequencies from the biblical text came later from the work of Dr. John Saba using a unique combination of the Menorah and the days of creation. Putting all this information together, I can say that there is a direct correlation between the Hebrew text or Hebrew characters and musical notes or frequencies.

This understanding has led to recording several CDs of the music of the Psalms of David which has been widely received around the world in at least 120 different countries. Most people who write indicate that they had a sense that there was a relationship, but they didn't know how to unlock it, and when they heard my recordings they knew that that was the music they had wanted to hear – it resonated in their spirits and stirred their souls. That alone would have been a real blessing, but YHVH had more for me to discover and understand.

The interesting thing I saw in the understanding of the frequencies coming from the book of Numbers is that this is the dedication of the completed wilderness Tabernacle. Detailed plans were given to Moses by YHVH while he was on Mt. Sinai. YHVH placed His Spirit into selected men and gave them wisdom and skill to be able to make the various pieces of furniture for the Tabernacle. Bezeliel was the chief craftsman in charge of carrying out the plans to exact specifications.

As my wife was studying this portion of scripture she asked me if I would do the "math thing" with the six articles of Tabernacle furniture and see if there was any relationship with the six articles of furniture and the six Solfeggio frequencies from Numbers 7. I was intrigued with the idea and started working out the musical mathematics. It was exciting to see the relationship come into focus; yes, there is an undeniable correlation! Each piece of Tabernacle furniture reveals a dominant Solfeggio frequency!

We began asking questions; were the frequencies given specifically as a part of the worship that was to be conducted in the Tabernacle? Was there something about the frequencies that was part of the protocol for coming into the presence of the Great I Am? Even if there is presently no Tabernacle is it possible that these frequencies could still be used today, as an enhancement to worship or a guide for coming into YHVH's presence?

In the Garden of Eden Adam and Eve were blessed with the privilege of meeting with YHVH in the cool of the evening and having conversation and building relationship with their Creator. When they sinned, that was one of the key things they lost. Ever since then, YHVH has placed into motion various ways of regaining that relationship through worship.

The Tabernacle of the Wilderness was one of those ways to help restore relationship with our Creator. Did not YHVH command Moses, "Let them make me a sanctuary that I may dwell among them." The Tabernacle was not just a collection of gold and silver, red, blue and purple material and animal skins and animal sacrifices. It was a pattern to be followed that brought the worshiper into contact with YHVH and presented a protocol that would ensure safety in doing so because of the shear energy of YHVH's presence.

The frequencies could actually be serving the purpose of bringing us into alignment with YHVH; or another way of putting it --- bringing us into frequency phase with our Creator. If we are out of phase, it produces "dis-ease" in us. If we are restored back into phase with our Creator, it brings health and life. Remember after presenting the blessings and the curses at the end of Deuteronomy, YHVH said, "Behold I present to you today, blessings and curses; life and death. Now behold, choose life and blessings." Life and blessings represent being in phase with YHVH. Death and curses represent being out of phase. Could the frequencies actually facilitate these blessings and life?

I will share a couple of anecdotal experiences with you to illustrate this. A couple of years back we were visiting a friend and noticed that she was playing my harp music softly in the background. A couple of hours later, we noticed that the music was still playing. Later on, it was still playing so I asked her if she might not be getting a little tired of the same music playing over and over. She replied, "Oh no, my days go so much better when this music is playing. I play it all the time now. It's not boring, it's a blessing."

Another time when my mother was in the hospital I took the harp into her room and played for her on and off throughout the day. As the nurses were preparing to change shifts, one of them came into the room and thanked me for the wonderful music. She went on to relate, "As you have been playing that music throughout the day, things have gone from chaos to calm; we haven't had such a relaxing day in as long as I have worked here and today was really rough until you started playing. Do you think you could come back tomorrow?"

As I started applying the method of bringing the Hebrew text into music that I had been using with the Psalms of David it quickly became apparent to me that the description of the Brazen Altar found in Exodus 27: 1-8 as taken from the Hebrew turned out to be the B chord for the word *altar* and the G chord for the word *brazen or copper*. Both of these chords were dominant in the chord progressions throughout the Hebrew text. This suggests very strongly a favoring of the 396 Hz Solfeggio frequency. This is the lowest frequency of the six and seemed like a good place to start, especially since this was the piece of furniture that was first encountered as one came into the Tabernacle compound.

Exodus 30: 17-21 describes the construction of the Laver. As the Hebrew chord progressions worked out, the G# chord was the chord for the word for Laver and again the word for Copper. This hinted strongly of the frequency of the Tabernacle of 417 Hz which is also the next rising frequency of the six Solfeggio frequencies. A pattern was emerging.

The text of Exodus 25:31-40 describes the making of the Menorah. In working out the chord progressions, the rising chord pattern of F – A – B – C shows up which strongly places it into the key of F which corresponds to the 528 Hz frequency which I call the creative, healing, miracle frequency. No wonder, because this is the Menorah – the Light of the World, Creator, Sustainer, Redeemer of all things!

In order to come into the presence of YHVH, the Tabernacle pattern indicates that we start at the lowest frequency, pausing at each article of furniture, contemplating the work that needs to be done in our lives in order to progress on to the next article of furniture. Each pause brings us to a higher frequency preparing us to stand before the Great King of the Universe. If we were going to visit the Queen of England we would have various people instructing us in the protocol of how to approach the queen – how much more the Great King of the Universe.

The Table of Showbread worked out to be the next higher frequency – 639 Hz from Exodus 25:23-30, and from Exodus 30:1-10 it was determined the next higher frequency of 741 Hz was the Altar of Incense.

Exodus 25:10-22 revealed the frequency of 852 Hz, the highest of the six Solfeggio frequencies. We have finally come to the Ark of the Covenant with its covering Cherubim over the Mercy Seat. True to the pattern of rising frequencies we now have the awesome and humbling opportunity to enter into the Shekinah presence of YHVH Tzvaot!

Each frequency addresses a different part of our being; the courtyard furniture represents cleansing and the Holy Place furniture represents refinement; different needs, different levels of intimacy; they all combine to bring us into YHVH's presence, restoring us into right relationship with our Creator.

I think it is important to understand that these frequencies of the Tabernacle are not just novelties to say we have another tidbit of knowledge to tuck away in our brains. These frequencies are actually imparting life to us because they are bringing us into the presence of our Creator, Sustainer, Redeemer. Without Him we are dead, even if we're still walking around. Knowledge is not going to save us. Only relationship with Him, our Abba, is going to bring us into His kingdom. We don't want to be standing at the door and hear Him say, "I'm sorry; I don't know you, depart from me." Only relationship, being in His presence will bring us into the wedding feast. It is my prayer that the music of these frequencies played on the harp and the meditations and prayers of this book will serve to help you come into that place of fellowship with YHVH Yashua so that you can ascend His Holy Mountain with clean hands and a pure heart.

Blessings!
Steve

Entering In

The wilderness tabernacle is a perfectly beautiful example of how our relationship is to be with Yashua. YHVH's original plan was to spend time with us – face to face – like He did with Adam and Eve when He came to talk with them in the cool of the day, Genesis 3:8. However, the adultery our first parents committed with hasatan in the paradise of YHVH called the Garden of Eden, ended our ability to be in the unveiled presence of YHVH's glory. Even Moses, of whom YHVH said He knew face to face, was not allowed to see the unveiled glory of YHVH lest he perish, Exodus 33:21-23. But Moses said in Deuteronomy 18:15, "YHVH your Elohe will raise up for you a prophet like me from among you, from your countrymen, you shall listen to him." Moses was prophesying the coming of the Word made flesh that was to dwell among us, Yashua, John 1:1-3. John 6:45-46 says, "It is written in the prophets, 'AND THEY SHALL ALL BE TAUGHT OF GOD.' Everyone who has heard and learned from the Father comes to Me. Not that anyone has seen the Father, except the One who is from God; He has seen the Father. 1John 4:14, We have seen and testify that the Father has sent the Son to be the Savior of the world. And John 14:9-11, Yashua said to him, "Have I been so long with you, and yet you have not come to know Me, Philip? He who has seen Me has seen the Father; how can you say, 'Show us the Father'? Do you not believe that I am in the Father, and the Father is in Me? The words that I say to you I do not speak on My own initiative, but the Father abiding in Me does His works. Believe Me that I am in the Father and the Father is in Me; otherwise believe because of the works themselves."

Just like the Word that became flesh and dwelt among us is Yashua so too the wilderness Tabernacle is a representation of Yashua; they both provide a way for restoration of relationship. The ancient Israelites attempted to have this relationship **through** faith, i.e., by keeping the letter of the Law. If we can keep the instructions of YHVH perfectly then we will be in a perfect relationship with YHVH. But, they could not because the Law of YHVH magnifies sin and sin leads to death. Yashua's redemptive work through His death and resurrection provide a way for us to be in relationship with YHVH **by** faith, i.e., not because of anything we do, for our righteousness is as filthy rags, but because of who Yashua is and our choice to let go of our rebellion and idolatry and abide under His perfect blood covering.

Rav Shaul said in his epistle to the congregation at Philippi chapter 2 verses 12 and 13, "So then, my beloved, just as you have always obeyed, not as in my presence only, but now much more in my absence, work out your salvation with fear and trembling; for it is God who is at work in you, both to will and to work for His good pleasure." So what is this working out of our salvation with fear and trembling that we are to do? This is the purpose of the Tabernacle from the perspective of the spirit of the Torah or law versus the letter of the Torah or law. Again Rav Shaul says in Romans 8:2-6, "For the law of the Spirit of life in Messiah Yashua has set you free from the law of sin and of death. For what the Law could not do, weak as it was through the flesh, God did: sending His own Son in the likeness of sinful flesh and as an offering for sin, He condemned sin in the flesh, so that the requirement of the Law might be fulfilled in us, who do not walk according to the flesh but according to the Spirit. For those who are according to the flesh set their minds on the things of the flesh, but those who are according to the Spirit, the things of the Spirit. <u>For the mind set on the flesh is death, but the mind set on the Spirit is life and peace...</u>" So <u>how do we live by the Spirit? By knowing the Word of YHVH, the Torah, which became flesh and dwelt among mankind</u>. The Torah, or the law, is the pathway we are to walk by the guidance of the Spirit of Truth which Yashua said He would send to us, John 16:13. This is working out our salvation with fear and trembling; walking the narrow path that leads to life. (Matthew 7:13-14)

The Tabernacle for the ancient Israelites was a physical manifestation of the presence of YHVH that they could interact with through the bringing of sacrifices and by the ministry of the priests and Levities; those specifically set aside to minister on behalf of the people before YHVH. As was mentioned earlier it was YHVH's plan to have face to face interaction with His people, but through our sin we caused a series of veils to come between us and YHVH. The first veil to come between us and face to face communion with YHVH was the holy Cherubim guarding the entrance to the Garden of Eden; we could no longer be in YHVH's paradise because mankind had chosen to hear and obey another god. The gateway veil of the Tabernacle is symbolic of entering YHVH's paradise, coming into His space to "hear and obey" Him. We come into His place with a sacrifice, an offering, a blood covering; for it is only by blood that we are covered and acceptable before YHVH; with Yashua's blood being the ultimate sacrifice.

The second veil was the death of Abel (Cain chose not to recognize "sin crouching at the door" and overcome it,) *Free Will* Genesis 4:6-8. It is through the Light of the World, which is Yashua, that we recognize sin; it is by eating of the Word of YHVH, the flesh and blood of Yashua, that we overcome sin and have life; it is in the sweet fragrance of His presence that our prayers ascend as acceptable pleas before the Throne of Grace.

The third veil was the extreme wickedness of mankind on the earth that caused YHVH to be grieved in his heart. He found only one man to minister before Him, Noah. At the death of Yashua on Calvary's stake, the third veil was torn in two making entry possible for all who believe on Him and come under His covering of blood. The sins of mankind down through the millennia have repeated the reinforcement of these veils until the time of Yashua's death on Calvary's stake. Now we choose to be, or not be, limited by the veils. Because of Yashua we have free access into YHVH's presence; as a child of the King and as the Bride of Yashua.

But there is a protocol for entering the presence of YHVH; protocol being a system of rules that explain the correct conduct and procedures to be followed in formal situations. Cleansing and refinement are what five of the six articles of Tabernacle furniture represent. According to the story of Queen Esther she spent six months with oil of myrrh and six months with spices and cosmetics before she was ready for her appointment with the king; should it be any less careful, thoughtful preparation for us?

*****

To be effective and fervent in prayer, a warrior in the kingdom of YHVH, we must become free of the accusations of hasatan. He is before the Throne of YHVH day and night accusing us of our sins, iniquities and transgressions and demanding that YHVH judge with justice. If we do not come before the Throne and present our case with "clean hands and a pure heart" the Righteous Judge will have no choice but to rule in hasatan's favor. Rav Shaul tells us in Ephesians 6:11-12 to, "Put on the full armor of God, so that you will be able to stand firm against the schemes of the devil. For our struggle is not against flesh and blood, but against the rulers, against the powers, against the world forces of this darkness, against the spiritual forces of wickedness in the heavenly places." If we are carrying unresolved sins, iniquities and transgressions that hasatan is constantly before the Throne accusing us of, and rightly so, we are guilty; how can we ever expect to war effectively in the Spirit realm on behalf of our bloodline and our brethren?

The Tabernacle was designed by YHVH for our benefit; to cleanse, refine and make us acceptable by way of the shed blood of Yashua to come into His presence, so we in turn may bring glory and honor and praise to His Name.

Yashua is our Mediator, it is recorded in **Revelation 3:5**, 'He who overcomes will thus be clothed in white garments; and I will not erase his name from the book of life, and I will confess his name before My Father and before His angels." Cleansing and refinement is part and parcel of becoming an overcomer. As an overcomer we stand at the Altar of Incense with our prayers and petitions and Yashua, our Mediator, says to YHVH, "Yes, they are cleansed, they are refined, I accept them," and The Father says, "Forgiven," and wipes our slate clean; and the mouth of the accuser is silenced. As this book progresses we will discuss this idea in greater detail.

It is our choice to make --- to become a living Tabernacle where YHVH dwells, or to remain outside the gate of the Holy City.

Revelation 22:14-15 Blessed are those who wash their robes, so that they may have the right to the tree of life, and may enter by the gates into the city. Outside are the dogs and the sorcerers and the immoral persons and the murderers and the idolaters, and everyone who loves and practices lying.

Revelation 21:27, and nothing unclean, and no one who practices abomination and lying, shall ever come into it, but only those whose names are written in the Lamb's book of life.

The ancient Israelites were instructed to build a Tabernacle for YHVH that He might dwell among them; the same is true for us today, YHVH desires to dwell in us!

1Peter 2:1-6 Therefore, putting aside all malice and all deceit and hypocrisy and envy and all slander, like newborn babies, long for the pure milk of the word, so that by it you may grow in respect to salvation, if you have tasted the kindness of YHVH. And coming to Him as to a living stone which has been rejected by men, but is choice and precious in the sight of God, you also, as living stones, are being built up as a spiritual house for a holy priesthood, to offer up spiritual sacrifices acceptable to God through Yashua haMashiach. For *this* is contained in Scripture: "BEHOLD, I LAY IN ZION A CHOICE STONE, A PRECIOUS CORNER *stone,* AND HE WHO BELIEVES IN HIM WILL NOT BE DISAPPOINTED."

Exodus 25:8 "Let them construct a sanctuary for Me, that I may dwell among them.

2Corinthians 6:14-18 Do not be bound together with unbelievers; for what partnership have righteousness and lawlessness, or what fellowship has light with darkness? Or what harmony has Christ with Belial, or what has a believer in common with an unbeliever? Or what agreement has the temple of God with idols? For we are the temple of the living God; just as God said, "I WILL DWELL IN THEM AND WALK AMONG THEM; AND I WILL BE THEIR GOD, AND THEY SHALL BE MY PEOPLE. Therefore, COME OUT FROM THEIR MIDST AND BE SEPARATE," says YHVH. AND DO NOT TOUCH WHAT IS UNCLEAN; and I will welcome you. And I will be a father to you, and you shall be sons and daughters to Me," says YHVH Almighty.

John 14:23 Yashua answered and said to him, "If anyone loves Me, he will keep My word; and My Father will love him, and We will come to him and make Our abode with him.

QUESTION: Do I want to be a Tabernacle where YHVH can dwell?

Song: *Lord, Prepare Me to be a Sanctuary* by Randy Rothwell

Enter in through the Gateway Veil leaving behind the world; choosing to begin your journey of cleansing.

When the first man and woman disobeyed the instructions of their Father, YHVH, they had to be put out of the Garden of Eden. Their disobedience put them in a place of darkness and Eden was a perfect place of LIGHT; darkness and LIGHT cannot share the same space --- turn on a light in a dark room and what happens to the darkness…it disappears! If we think of the Tree of Life as Yashua our Messiah and the Garden of Eden as the wedding chamber, then Adam and Eve, when they listened to the serpent and ate from the Tree of the Knowledge of Good and Evil committed adultery against their Bridegroom, Yashua. **Genesis 3:22-23** Then YHVH God said, "Behold, the man has become like one of Us, knowing good and evil; and now, he might stretch out his hand, and take also from the tree of life, and eat, and live forever"-- therefore YHVH God sent him out from the garden of Eden, to cultivate the ground from which he was taken.

According to Torah instruction…

Deuteronomy 24:1 "When a man takes a wife and marries her, and it happens that she finds no favor in his eyes because he has found some indecency in her, and he writes her a certificate of divorce and puts *it* in her hand and sends her out from his house…

Matthew 5:31 "It was said, 'WHOEVER SENDS HIS WIFE AWAY, LET HIM GIVE HER A CERTIFICATE OF DIVORCE'…

Jeremiah 3:6-18 Then YHVH said to me in the days of Josiah the king, "Have you seen what faithless Israel did? She went up on every high hill and under every green tree, and she was a harlot there. I thought, 'After she has done all these things she will return to Me'; but she did not return, and her treacherous sister Judah saw it. And I saw that for all the adulteries of faithless Israel, I had sent her away and given her a writ of divorce, yet her treacherous sister Judah did not fear; but she went and was a harlot also. Because of the lightness of her harlotry, she polluted the land and committed adultery with stones and trees. Yet in spite of all this her treacherous sister Judah did not return to Me with all her heart, but rather in deception," declares YHVH. And

YHVH said to me, "Faithless Israel has proved herself more righteous than treacherous Judah. Go and proclaim these words toward the north and say, 'Return, faithless Israel,' declares YHVH; 'I will not look upon you in anger. For I am gracious,' declares YHVH; 'I will not be angry forever. 'Only acknowledge your iniquity, that you have transgressed against YHVH your God and have scattered your favors to the strangers under every green tree, and you have not obeyed My voice,' declares YHVH. 'Return, O faithless sons,' declares YHVH; 'For I am a master to you, and I will take you one from a city and two from a family, and I will bring you to Zion. Then I will give you shepherds after My own heart, who will feed you on knowledge and understanding. It shall be in those days when you are multiplied and increased in the land," declares YHVH, "they will no longer say, 'The ark of the covenant of YHVH.' And it will not come to mind, nor will they remember it, nor will they miss *it,* nor will it be made again. "At that time they will call Jerusalem 'The Throne of YHVH' and all the nations will be gathered to it, to Jerusalem, for the name of YHVH; nor will they walk anymore after the stubbornness of their evil heart. In those days the house of Judah will walk with the house of Israel, and they will come together from the land of the north to the land that I gave your fathers as an inheritance."

The Gateway Veil of the Tabernacle symbolizes the separation between us and YHVH that took place when

Adam and Eve were sent out from the Garden. YHVH stationed at the east end of Eden the cherubim and the flaming sword which turned every direction to guard the way to the Tree of Life. (Gen 3:24) <u>The Tabernacle, which was always pitched with the Gateway Veil facing east, has now become an invitation to enter back into YHVH's time and space</u>.

Isaiah 58:11 "And YHVH will continually guide you, And satisfy your desire in scorched places, And give strength to your bones; and you will be like a watered garden, and like a spring of water whose waters do not fail.

Jeremiah 31:12 "They will come and shout for joy on the height of Zion, and they will be radiant over the bounty of YHVH-- over the grain and the new wine and the oil, and over the young of the flock and the herd; and their life will be like a watered garden, and they will never languish again.

As you contemplate entering through the first veil preparing to offer sacrifices on the Brazen Altar and wash in the Laver keep these five admonitions in mind --- adapted from Dr. Michael Brown's article in www.charismanews.com (8.2015), ***5 Lessons From the Hacking of an Adultery Website.***

Sooner or later, your sin will find you out (Num. 32:23). Whether in this world or the world to come, if we don't turn from our sins and renounce them, they will catch up with us and find us out. Count on it.

2. Nothing is hidden from God. The real folly of "secret" sin is that it's not secret at all, and the one whose opinion matters most is the one who sees it all. God sees what we do in secret...

3. It pays to live clean. When you have nothing to hide, you gladly come into the light (John 3:21), and when your conscience is clean, you have confidence before

God and man. What price will you put on a clean conscience?

4. Be quick to repent. If we try to cover our sins we will not succeed; if we confess and forsake them, we will find mercy (Prov. 28:13). The temptation, of course, is to cover one sin with another sin; when we add sin to sin, we only compound our difficulties.

5. God's Word is eternally relevant. As it is written in Proverbs 6, "Can a man take fire in his bosom, and his clothes not be burned? Can one walk upon hot coals, and his feet not be burned?"

His abundant mercy is waiting for you, and the godly sorrow you experience today will lead to freedom and joy tomorrow.

DEFINITIONS to keep in mind as you prepare to enter the Tabernacle:

Sin --- is lawlessness as in habitually breaking the law, but it is something that can be ruled over. If one does not rule over sin, i.e. bringing lawless tendencies into submission, James 1:14-15 speaks of the end result; "But each one is tempted when he is carried away and enticed by his own lust. Then when lust has conceived, it gives birth to sin; and when sin is accomplished, it brings forth death."

Iniquity --- perverse or morally evil; idolatry as in the serving of other gods living in opposition to YHVH's Word. Iniquity abounds or increases as it passes from generation to generation.

Transgression --- to revolt or break away from constituted authority; rebellion as in defiance or resistance to authority.

We have all sinned and fallen short of the glory of YHVH. (Romans 3:23) Sin is what separates us from YHVH. To come back into relationship with our Creator we must be cleansed of our sins, iniquities and transgressions. The Brazen Altar and the Laver in the courtyard of the Tabernacle represent this cleansing process.

QUESTION: Are you ready to submit all of you to YHVH's cleansing process?

Song: *Pure Bride* by Leeland

The Brazen Altar

The frequency associated with the brazen altar is 396hz, the color is red and it is associated with expanding your awareness, undoing situations and facilitating change.

Song: *Awakening* by Chris Tomlin

Exodus 27:1-8 "And you shall make the altar of acacia wood, five cubits long and five cubits wide; the altar shall be square, and its height shall be three cubits. You shall make its horns on its four corners; its horns shall be of one piece with it, and you shall overlay it with bronze. You shall make its pails for removing its ashes, and its shovels and its basins and its forks and its firepans; you shall make all its utensils of bronze. You shall make for it a grating of network of bronze, and on the net you shall make four bronze rings at its four corners. You shall put it beneath, under the ledge of the altar, so that the net will reach halfway up the altar. You shall make poles for the altar, poles of acacia wood, and overlay them with bronze.

Its poles shall be inserted into the rings, so that the poles shall be on the two sides of the altar when it is carried. You shall make it hollow with planks; as it was shown to you in the mountain, so they shall make it."

Ever since the first man and woman sinned in the Garden of Eden the human race has been beset by accusations from the 'accuser of the brethren', hasatan. The first accusation by the accuser was to call YHVH a liar and promote doubt about YHVH in the heart of mankind; Genesis 3:4-5, The serpent said to the woman, "You surely will not die! For God knows that in the day you eat from it your eyes will be opened, and you will be like God, knowing good and evil." Mankind has lived under the affliction of this doubt ever since; does YHVH really love me, does He really hear me, does He really care about my life, my family, my circumstances? From the first man and woman this seed of doubt has carried down the generational bloodlines to you. From this seed of doubt has grown up and passed down to you all manner of sin and iniquity and unrighteousness. As you begin your journey through the Tabernacle ask YHVH to highlight to you the iniquities and transgressions in your bloodline that you need to recognize, take responsibility for, repent of, renounce their hold on you and your family, ask to be removed, resist the temptation to invite them back by indulging in old behaviors, rejoice that Yashua has vindicated you by covering you with His blood and ask for and accept His restoration.

This first piece of furniture in the Tabernacle is most often the hardest one to truly deal with; we have a tendency to 'play' with it or ignore it. It's in the courtyard after all --- I want to get on to the good stuff inside the tent. No matter how enticing it may seem to get on with this journey and get inside the tent you, very likely, will be consumed like Nadab and Abihu because you will have entered with strange fire if you do not practice due diligence with the courtyard furniture. YHVH Yashua is pure LIGHT. Darkness cannot abide in light. If there is darkness in you that darkness will have to disappear before the light. Proverbs 16:17-18, "The highway of the upright is to depart from evil; he who watches his way preserves his life.

Pride *goes* before destruction, And a haughty spirit before stumbling." The hardest thing to do is to give up everything; hold nothing back, lie down on the altar and allow yourself to truly die. Abraham was willing to sacrifice his only son, Isaac and Isaac was willing to allow himself to be sacrificed, trusting that YHVH had a plan for greater glory. Are you willing to trust this completely with the full assurance that YHVH Yashua has a plan for greater glory for you as well?

You might be tempted to think at this point; "I go into YHVH's presence all the time and I don't do all this due diligence stuff. He hears me, He answers me, He talks to me; I feel His presence surrounding me during times of praise and worship; what's the big deal, He knows my heart?"

The "big deal" is **Deuteronomy 13:1-4** "If a prophet or a dreamer of dreams arises among you and gives you a sign or a wonder, and the sign or the wonder comes true, concerning which he spoke to you, saying, 'Let us go after other gods (whom you have not known) and let us serve them,' you shall not listen to the words of that prophet or that dreamer of dreams; for YHVH your God is testing you to find out if you love YHVH your God with all your heart and with all your soul. You shall follow YHVH your God and fear Him; and you shall keep His commandments, listen to His voice, serve Him, and cling to Him."

Hasatan is the master of deception and YHVH allows this according to the above scripture to test us. Beware friend, hasatan goes about like a roaring lion seeking whom he can find to devour.

The prophet Jeremiah records the words of YHVH about our heart in chapter 17:9-10, "The heart is more deceitful than all else and is desperately, sick; who can understand it? I, YHVH, search the heart, I test the mind, even to give to each man according to his ways, according to the results of his deeds."

Yes, He does know our hearts.

His will, or do I really only want His approval and blessing for my way?

Whole Burnt offering --- Leviticus 1:2-9, "Speak to the sons of Israel and say to them, 'When any man of you brings an offering to YHVH, you shall bring your offering of animals from the herd or the flock. 'If his offering is a burnt offering from the herd, he shall offer it, a male without defect; he shall offer it at the doorway of the tent of meeting, that he may be accepted before YHVH. 'He shall lay his hand on the head of the burnt offering, that it may be accepted for him to make atonement on his behalf. 'He shall slay the young bull before YHVH; and Aaron's sons the priests shall offer up the blood and sprinkle the blood around on the altar that is at the doorway of the tent of meeting. 'He shall then skin the burnt offering and cut it into its pieces. 'The sons of Aaron the priest shall put fire on the altar and arrange wood on the fire. 'Then Aaron's sons the priests shall arrange the pieces, the head and the suet over the wood which is on the fire that is on the altar. 'Its entrails, however, and its legs he shall wash with water. And the priest shall offer up in smoke all of it on the altar for a burnt offering, an offering by fire of a soothing aroma to YHVH."

(handwritten top right: Doorway – Altar. Covenant is formed)

The whole burnt offering is our opportunity to enter the courtroom of heaven and confess that, yes, I, and my bloodline are guilty of _____. I and my bloodline deserve punishment. I am laying myself on the altar as a whole burnt offering for myself and my bloodline; take all of me, there is nothing good in me, or my bloodline, forgive me and my bloodline for _____. And then allow the shed blood of Yashua to cover you and your bloodline and make you and your bloodline an acceptable offering before YHVH. He takes our sin, all the way back to the first man and woman, and wipes this sin off our account. The accuser of the brethren has no more legal right to continue to accuse you; you have been forgiven and cleansed of your iniquity.

(handwritten margin notes: Altar of Sacrifice ↓ Remove enemy authority)

> **Prayer:** Abba, I really blew it! I slandered, maligned, gossiped, engaged in verbal abuse; I participated in immorality, impurity, sensuality, idolatry, sorcery, enmities, strife, jealousy, outbursts of anger, disputes, dissensions, factions, envying, drunkenness, carousing, and worse... Romans 7:15-19, for what I am doing, I do not understand; for I am not practicing what I would like to do, but I am doing the very thing I hate. But if I do the very thing I do not want to do, I agree with the Law, confessing that the Law is good. So now, no longer am I the one doing it, but sin which dwells in me. For I know that

nothing good dwells in me, that is, in my flesh; for the willing is present in me, but the doing of the good is not. For the good that I want, I do not do, but I practice the very evil that I do not want. Rom 7:24, Wretched person that I am! Who will set me free from the body of this death? Rom 7:25, Thanks be to God through Yashua haMashiach our Adonai!

Rom 8:1-4, Therefore there is now no condemnation for those who are in Messiah Yashua. For the law of the Spirit of life in Messiah Yashua has set you free from the law of sin and of death. For what the Law could not do, weak as it was through the flesh, God did: sending His own Son in the likeness of sinful flesh and as an offering for sin, He condemned sin in the flesh, so that the requirement of the Law might be fulfilled in us, who do not walk according to the flesh but according to the Spirit.

Thank you Abba, for this "do over", my opportunity to give up all of myself to You and be re-made on Your Potter's wheel; a vessel fit for Your use.

Isaiah 64:5-9 You meet him who rejoices in doing righteousness, who remembers You in Your ways. Behold, You were angry, for we sinned, w*e continued* in them a long time; and shall we be saved?

For all of us have become like one who is unclean, and all our righteous deeds are like a filthy garment; and all of us wither like a leaf, and our iniquities, like the wind, take us away. There is no one who calls on Your name, who arouses himself to take hold of You; for You have hidden Your face from us and have delivered us into the power of our iniquities. But now, O YHVH, You are our Father, we are the clay, and You our potter; and all of us are the work of Your hand. Do not be angry beyond measure, O YHVH, nor remember iniquity forever; behold, look now, all of us are Your people.

2Corinthians 4:6-10 For God, who said, "Light shall shine out of darkness," is the One who has shone in our hearts to give the Light of the knowledge of the glory of God in the face of Messiah. But we have this treasure in earthen vessels, so that the surpassing greatness of the power will be of God and not from ourselves; *we are* afflicted in every way, but not crushed; perplexed, but not despairing; persecuted, but not forsaken; struck down, but not destroyed; always carrying about in the body the dying of Yashua, so that the life of Yashua also may be manifested in our body.

Offering yourself as a whole burnt offering is an opportunity for restoration, deliverance, and healing, cleansing and new life!

Psalm 103:10-13, "He has not dealt with us according to our sins, nor rewarded us according to our iniquities. For as high as the heavens are above the earth, so great is His lovingkindness toward those who fear Him. As far as the east is from the west, so far has He removed our transgressions from us. Just as a father has compassion on his children, so YHVH has compassion on those who fear Him."

YHVH gives us the opportunity to have a "do over" by dying to our unholy, unrighteous thoughts, attitudes, actions and behaviors daily; everything offered up in smoke as a soothing aroma to YHVH. Why are whole burnt offerings a soothing aroma to YHVH? Is it because our sin of rebellion and idolatry are consumed in the fire leaving nothing but ashes for hasatan!

Romans 8:35-39 Who will separate us from the love of Messiah? Will tribulation, or distress, or persecution, or famine, or nakedness, or peril, or sword? Just as it is written, "FOR YOUR SAKE WE ARE BEING PUT TO DEATH ALL DAY LONG; WE WERE CONSIDERED AS SHEEP TO BE SLAUGHTERED." But in all these things we overwhelmingly conquer through Him who loved us. For I am convinced that neither death, nor life, nor angels, nor principalities, nor things present, nor things to come, nor powers, nor height, nor depth, nor any other created thing, will be able to separate us from the love of God, which is in Yashua haMashiach our Adonai.

Titus 3:3-7 For we also once were foolish ourselves, disobedient, deceived, enslaved to various lusts and pleasures, spending our life in malice and envy, hateful, hating one another. But when the kindness of God our Savior and *His* love for mankind appeared, He saved us, not on the basis of deeds which we have done in righteousness, but according to His mercy, by the washing of regeneration and renewing by the Holy Spirit, whom He poured out upon us richly through Yashua haMashiach our Savior, so that being justified by His grace we would be made heirs according to *the* hope of eternal life.

Leviticus 11:45, 'For I am YHVH who brought you up from the land of Egypt to be your God; thus you shall be holy, for I am holy.'"

Peace offerings --- **Leviticus 3:1** "'Now if his offering is a sacrifice of peace offerings, if he is going to offer out of the herd, whether male or female, he shall offer it without defect before YHH. 'He shall lay his hand on the head of his offering and slay it at the doorway of the tent of meeting, and Aaron's sons the priests shall sprinkle the blood around on the altar. 'From the sacrifice of the peace offerings he shall present an offering by fire to YHVH, the fat that covers the entrails and all the fat that is on the entrails, and the two kidneys with the fat that is on them, which is on the loins, and the lobe of the liver, which he shall remove with the kidneys. 'Then Aaron's sons shall offer it up in smoke on the altar on the burnt offering, which is on the wood that is on the fire; it is an offering by fire of a soothing aroma to YHVH."

When we need a whole burnt offering "do over" we most likely have allowed our shalom to be severely assaulted; a definition of shalom being; YHVH's power that destroys the one that brings chaos; whether it be in us, our home, workplace, or with our family and friends; our thoughts, behavior, attitudes and actions have been such that we have attracted hasatan and not YHVH. It is the Priest's job to offer atonement for the penitent one. The sacrifice of "all of me" as a whole burnt offering allows Yashua to put His Hand over the mouth of the accuser of the brethren, hasatan. "Shhh!" He says, "you may not say one more word against her/him, they are covered!"

YHVH wants all the fat! In our bodies we burn fat for energy; YHVH says give all the fat to Me. This is a representation of giving to YHVH the energy we spend in destructive endeavors that do not promote Shalom. YHVH wants the fat to remind us to work the muscles of our heart to love our fellow brethren, work the muscles of our diaphragm to speak words of encouragement, edification and exhortation, work the muscles of our hands and feet to feed the hungry, clothe the naked, visit the sick and those in prison.

> **Prayer:** Abba, forgive me for allowing the one who is in this world to steal your gift of shalom from me. I thank you for Your promise that You are in me and You are greater than he that is in the world and that You are working out Your will in my life. I lay my peace offering; the energy I

expended for unholy and unrighteous actions, on my whole burnt offering which is all of me. Please accept my offering and may it ascend as a soothing aroma before You.

Grain Offering --- Leviticus 2:1 'Now when anyone presents a grain offering as an offering to YHVH, his offering shall be of fine flour, and he shall pour oil on it and put frankincense on it. Lev 2:2, 'He shall then bring it to Aaron's sons the priests; and shall take from it his handful of its fine flour and of its oil with all of its frankincense. And the priest shall offer it up in smoke as its memorial portion on the altar, an offering by fire of a soothing aroma to YHVH. Lev 2:13 'Every grain offering of yours, moreover, you shall season with salt, so that the salt of the covenant of your God shall not be lacking from your grain offering; with all your offerings you shall offer salt.

The story of David's sin with Bathsheba which led to the willful murder of her husband Uriah in his attempt to cover up his sin was intentional. There is no sacrifice for intentional sin; we must bear the consequences or pay the penalty for this sin. The consequence of David's intentional sin was delivered to him by the prophet Nathan.

2Samuel 12:10-14, 'Now therefore, the sword shall never depart from your house, because you have despised Me and have taken the wife of Uriah the Hittite to be your wife.' "Thus says YHVH, 'Behold, I will raise up evil against you from your own household; I will even take your wives before your eyes and give *them* to your companion, and he will lie with your wives in broad daylight. 'Indeed you did it secretly, but I will do this thing before all Israel, and under the sun.'" Then David said to Nathan, "I have sinned against YHVH." And Nathan said to David, "YHVH also has taken away your sin; you shall not die. However, because by this deed you have given occasion to the enemies of YHVH to blaspheme, the child also that is born to you shall surely die."

When David was confronted by the prophet Nathan concerning his intentional sin, his response was immediate and profound as found in Psalm 51:17, "The sacrifices of God are a broken spirit; a broken and a contrite heart, O God, You will not despise." Broken and contrite are two words that express the spiritual significance of the grain offering; the whole grain is broken and contrited, or crushed fine. When we, like David, have sinned, then tried to cover up that sin YHVH will allow circumstances to break us and crush us until like David we say;

Oh Abba, Be gracious to me, according to Your lovingkindness; according to the greatness of Your compassion blot out my transgressions. Wash me thoroughly from my iniquity and cleanse me from my sin; for I know my transgressions, and my sin is ever before me. Purify me with hyssop, and I shall be clean; wash me, and I shall be whiter than snow. Make me to hear joy and gladness, let the bones which You have broken rejoice. Hide Your face from my sins and blot out all my iniquities. Create in me a clean heart, O God, and renew a steadfast spirit within me. Do not cast me away from Your presence and do not take Your Holy Spirit from me. Restore to me the joy of Your salvation and sustain me with a willing spirit. (quoting portions of Psalm 51)

> **Prayer:** Forgive me Abba, for those I have sinned against. Yashua said "You are the salt of the earth; Mat 5:13, but if the salt has become tasteless, how can it be made salty again? It is no longer good for anything, except to be thrown out and trampled underfoot by men."
>
> Abba, crush me, bruise me, break me, if this is what it takes to deliver me from my sin of _____. I do not want to be thrown out of Your kingdom.

And the unleavened cake was to be mixed with oil which reminds me of the scripture from Psalm 133:

Behold, how good and how pleasant it is for brethren to dwell together in unity! It is like the precious oil upon the head, coming down upon the beard, even Aaron's beard, coming down upon the edge of his robes. It is like the dew of Hermon coming down upon the mountains of

Zion; for there YHVH commanded the blessing---life forever.

Olive oil undergoes a vigorous process of crushing, straining and refinement before it is deemed usable. To dwell together in unity we also must be crushed, strained of impurities and refined. And isn't this the purpose of the Tabernacle; cleansing, refinement, dwelling in unity with YHVH, to be holy as He is holy.

And frankincense was to be added to the unleavened cake spread with oil. In the ancient world, there were few items considered to be of greater worth and value than frankincense. For this reason, pure frankincense was often referred to as "liquid gold" and was a highly prized commodity for trade and commerce.

The grain offering was an unleavened cake of fine flour spread with oil and offered with frankincense as a soothing aroma to YHVH. This offering had great cost; it not only involved grinding to a fine powder the grain and crushing the olives for the oil, but also parting with a precious commodity.

David's sin with Bathsheba involved a great cost --- the life of his infant son. What has your intentional sin cost you? Pay the price, resist living in the past, and move on into greater realms of glory with YHVH Yashua!

> **Prayer**: Abba help me, I pray, to live a life broken and ground fine before you, (1Pe 2:5) as a living

stone, in unity with other living stones, built up as a spiritual house for a holy priesthood, so that I might offer up spiritual sacrifices acceptable to You through Yashua haMashiach. I relinquish all of the things I hold of most worldly value and give them to You so that I may be pure and holy before You.

Guilt Offering --- Lev 6:2-7, "When a person sins and acts unfaithfully against YHVH, and deceives his companion in regard to a deposit or a security entrusted to him, or through robbery, or if he has extorted from his companion, or has found what was lost and lied about it and sworn falsely, so that he sins in regard to any one of the things a man may do; then it shall be, when he sins and becomes guilty, that he shall restore what he took by robbery or what he got by extortion, or the deposit which was entrusted to him or the lost thing which he found, or anything about which he swore falsely; he shall make restitution for it in full and add to it one-fifth more. He shall give it to the one to whom it belongs on the day he presents his guilt offering. "Then he shall bring to the priest his guilt offering to YHVH, a ram without defect from the flock, according to your valuation, for a guilt offering, and the priest shall make atonement for him before YHVH, and he will be forgiven for any one of the things which he may have done to incur guilt."

The guilt offering requires something from you; it requires restitution.

Full Definition of RESTITUTION

1: an act of restoring or a condition of being restored: as, a) a restoration of something to its rightful owner, b) a making good of or giving an equivalent for some injury
2: a legal action serving to cause restoration of a previous state

Guilt is like a festering wound; it is a bad feeling caused by knowing or thinking that you have done something bad or wrong. You can try to clear your conscience by bringing to the altar the sacrifice --- offering all of yourself as a whole burnt offering, but the matter will not be internally resolved for you until restitution is made. You will just smolder on the altar of your conscience, like a festering wound, you can try to cover the wound with a bandage, but until restitution is made no true healing will happen. The wound will grow until it consumes you, dictating your thoughts, behaviors, attitudes and actions. YHVH is not glorified or honored with the offering we place before Him if restitution is not made on the day you bring your guilt offering before YHVH.

> **Prayer**: Abba, forgive me for thinking I could hide anything from you; and thank you for not allowing me to presume that I could hide anything from you! I have sinned against You, whether my sin was intentional or not makes no difference. You want me to be holy as You are holy, therefore I confess my wrong-doing to

_____ and ask you to forgive me. I have gone to _____ and I have made restitution and asked for their forgiveness. Please accept this offering that I now place before you; all of me. Take me, cleanse me, wash me whiter than snow with the shed blood of Yashua; for it is under His blood covering that I want to abide and I know that rebellion and idolatry are darkness and darkness cannot abide in the Light. I want to live in Your Light. Thank you for accepting my sacrifice and cleansing me of my guilt in this matter with _____.

The Laver

The frequency associated with the laver is 417hz, the color is orange and it is associated with liberating guilt and fear.

Song: *O The Blood* by Gateway Worship

Exodus 30:17-21 The LORD spoke to Moses, saying, "You shall also make a laver of bronze, with its base of bronze, for washing; and you shall put it between the tent of meeting and the altar, and you shall put water in it. Aaron and his sons shall wash their hands and their feet from it; when they enter the tent of meeting, they shall wash with water, so that they will not die; or when they approach the altar to minister, by offering up in smoke a fire *sacrifice* to YHVH. So they shall wash their hands and their feet, so that they will not die; and it shall be a perpetual statute for them, for Aaron and his descendants throughout their generations."

Even though the Laver is the second piece of furniture that is encounter in the courtyard of the Tabernacle it is used twice by the priests; once before offering any sacrifices and then again before entering the tent of the Tabernacle. The Laver represents a separation of the holy from the profane or common.

*We are attracted to YHVH or we are attracted to hasatan. We can repel YHVH or we can repel hasatan; either one by our actions, thoughts, attitudes and behaviors. One aspect then of the Laver is for washing away sweat --- the labor of our work, the curse from the fall --- so we can come into YHVH's presence for scripture states in **Ezekiel 44:18**,that the priests were not to put anything on their body that would make them sweat.*

Genesis 3:16-19, To the woman He said, "I will greatly multiply Your pain in childbirth, In pain you will bring forth children; yet your desire will be for your husband, and he will rule over you." Then to Adam He said, "Because you have listened to the voice of your wife, and have eaten from the tree about which I commanded you, saying, 'You shall not eat from it'; cursed is the ground because of you; Ii toil you will eat of it all the days of your life. Both thorns and thistles it shall grow for you; and you will eat the plants of the field; by the sweat of your face You will eat bread, till you return to the ground, because from it you were taken; for you are dust, and to dust you shall return."

The first washing in the Laver is for the purpose of setting one's self apart from the common or everyday and entering into the sacred or holy activity of ministry on behalf of the people before YHVH.

John 13:5-12, tells the story of Yashua with a towel and a basin of water. He comes to His disciples as a servant to wash their feet and tells him, "What I'm doing for you, you will not understand now. Afterward you will understand." Peter resists this act of service by his Adonai with these words, "You shall never wash my feet. "Yashua answers him by saying, "Peter, if you do not allow this you have no share with Me in My kingdom." Simon Peter answers back, "Adonai, not my feet only but also my hands and my head. " Yashua said, "He that is washed does not need to be washed again except for his feet." When he had washed their feet and put on His outer garments, He resumed his place and asked them, "Do you understand what I have done to you?"

Yashua's last words to His disciples as recorded by Matthew are, "Go therefore and make disciples of all nations." Washing their feet was Yashua's way of saying, "I am separating you from the profane unto the holy; now go into the entire world and every place the sole of your foot treads is going to be a possession for the kingdom of YHVH."

It was a fulfillment for those disciples of what He had told Abraham, Moshe and Joshua. What did his disciples do?

They went into the entire world with the gospel. Now every time you have an opportunity to wash feet, do it with the same understanding. It's a separating out; it's purification; it's like Yashua saying, "I don't want you to go into the world with your profanity or your faults, troubles or your agenda. I want you separated out for Me; holy to Me, holy as I am holy and where you go you will take it as My possession."

The Laver symbolizes cleansing; separating the holy from the profane or common. Yashua was preparing His disciples for the great commission.

Matthew 28:18-20 "And Jesus came up and spoke to them, saying, 'All authority has been given to Me in heaven and on earth. Go therefore and make disciples of all the nations, baptizing them in the name of the Father and the Son and the Holy Spirit, teaching them to observe all that I commanded you; and lo, I am with you always, even to the end of the age.'"

And so with us too!

> **Prayer**: Abba, it is my desire to lay down my needs, my wants and my desires; the work of my hands, so that I might focus on Your wonderful face. I am really striving, worried, angry, fearful about _____. As I come to the laver please
>
> wash the "sweat" of my strife, worry, anger, fear from me that I may enter Your presence with

rejoicing. Forgive me for taking up burdens that I have allowed to oppress me; for holding onto them and not releasing them to You. I want to perfectly reflect Yashua's image. Purify me as Your word says in Malachi 3:3, You will sit as a smelter and purifier of silver, and You will purify the sons of Levi and refine them like gold and silver, so that they may present to YHVH offerings in righteousness. (Psa 51:2), Wash me thoroughly from my iniquity and cleanse me from my sin. (Psa 51:7), Purify me with hyssop, and I shall be clean; wash me, and I shall be whiter than snow. (Psa 51:10-12), Create in me a clean heart, O God, and renew a steadfast spirit within me. Do not cast me away from Your presence and do not take Your Holy Spirit from me. Restore to me the joy of Your salvation and sustain me with a willing spirit.

Matthew 11:28-30, "Come to Me, all who are weary and heavy-laden, and I will give you rest. Take My yoke upon you and learn from Me, for I am gentle and humble in heart, and YOU WILL FIND REST FOR YOUR SOULS. For My yoke is easy and My burden is light."

The second time the priests used the laver was before they entered into the tent of the Tabernacle to minister before YHVH. They washed in the blood of the sacrifice just as we are washed in the blood of the Lamb, Yashua. It is only under the blood covering of Yashua that we can enter into the presence of YHVH. As the priests washed the blood of the sacrifices from their hands and feet into the water of the Laver they witnessed the clear water turn blood red --- a visual reminder that Yashua's blood cleanses us from all sin. It is cleansed from our sin that we now enter the veil into the Holy Place of the Tabernacle.

Have you allowed the Blood of the Lamb, Yashua to cover and cleanse you?

> **Prayer:** Abba, I am so humbled by your sacrifice on Calvary's stake; the blood you shed for my deliverance from the bondage of the evil one. How lightly I have esteemed this most precious of gifts, Your blood. For it is only as I abide under Your shed blood am I seen perfect in the eyes of YHVH. It is only as I am washed in Your blood that I able to come into the presence of the Great I AM. (Rev 7:13-17), Then one of the elders answered, saying to me, "These who are clothed in the white robes, who are they, and where have they come from?" I said to him, "My lord, you know." And he said to me, "These are the ones who come out of the great tribulation, and they have washed their robes and made them white in the blood of the Lamb. For this reason, they are before the throne of God; and they serve Him day and night in His temple; and He who sits on the throne will spread His tabernacle

over them. They will hunger no longer, nor thirst anymore; nor will the sun beat down on them, nor any heat; for the Lamb in the center of the throne will be their shepherd, and will guide them to springs of the water of life; and God will wipe every tear from their eyes."

O Abba, do not allow me to leave this Laver until I am washed thoroughly in Your blood, cleanse me please, of all my unrighteousness. Bring to my mind what I may still need to offer up as a sacrifice to You so that the enemy of the brethren has no legal right to continue to accuse me or my household of any unrighteousness.

The story in Ezekiel 16 about Jerusalem is a parallel to each of our lives; we were born in iniquity, the accuser of the brethren is accusing us before the throne of YHVH day and night (Rev 12:10), Then I heard a loud voice in heaven, saying, "Now the salvation, and the power, and the kingdom of our God and the authority of His Christ have come, for the accuser of our brethren has been thrown down, he who accuses them before our God day and night." But we overcome him because of the blood of the Lamb and because of the word of our testimony, and that we do not love our life even when faced with death.

It is the blood of the Lamb, Yashua, that cleanses us. When we are cleansed by Yashua He adorns us with His splendor, as His Bride, His emissary to the nations. Let us be faithful to Him, even unto death.

Ezekiel 16:4-14, "As for your birth, on the day you were born your navel cord was not cut, nor were you washed with water for cleansing; you were not rubbed with salt or even wrapped in cloths. No eye looked with pity on you to do any of these things for you, to have compassion on you. Rather you were thrown out into the open field, for you were abhorred on the day you were born."

"When I passed by you and saw you squirming in your blood, I said to you *while you were* in your blood, 'Live!' Yes, I said to you *while you were* in your blood, 'Live!'

"I made you numerous like plants of the field. Then you grew up, became tall and reached the age for fine ornaments; *your* breasts were formed and your hair had grown. Yet you were naked and bare.

"Then I passed by you and saw you, and behold, you were at the time for love; so I spread My skirt over you and covered your nakedness. I also swore to you and entered into a covenant with you so that you became Mine," declares the YHVH GOD.

"Then I bathed you with water, washed off your blood from you and anointed you with oil. I also clothed you with embroidered cloth and put sandals of porpoise skin on your feet; and I wrapped you with fine linen and covered you with silk. I adorned you with ornaments, put bracelets on your hands and a necklace around your neck. I also put a ring in your nostril, earrings in your ears and a beautiful crown on your head. Thus you were adorned with gold and silver, and your dress was of fine linen, silk and embroidered cloth. You ate fine flour, honey and oil; so you were exceedingly beautiful and advanced to royalty.

Then your fame went forth among the nations on account of your beauty, for it was perfect because of My splendor which I bestowed on you," declares the YHVH GOD."

> **Prayer:** Oh Abba, it is my greatest need to be the beautiful bride of Yashua! I pray that I would be found separated from the iniquity of Babylon; that I would "Come out of her, my people, so that you will not participate in her sins and receive of her plagues..." (Rev 18:4).
>
> I pray that every sin, iniquity, transgression, curse that has ever occurred in my bloodline be forgiven, washed from me, erased from the pages of my life and the life of my bloodline that I and my household might be pure and spotless before You. Truly Abba, may the world know
>
> that we are Your bride by the love we have for one another!

The Second Veil --- the Bride of Yashua makes herself ready by working out her salvation with fear and trembling. Philippians 2:12-15, "So then, my beloved, just as you have always obeyed, not as in my presence only, but now much more in my absence, work out your salvation with fear and trembling; for it is God who is at work in you, both to will and to work for His good pleasure. Do all things without grumbling or disputing; so that you will prove yourselves to be blameless and innocent, children of God above reproach in the midst of a crooked and perverse generation, among who you appear as lights in the world..."

Going beyond the second veil into the Holy Place represents our decision to have our character refined. The Menorah, Table of Showbread, and the Incense Altar are all designed to teach us how to be overcomers of our sins, iniquities and transgressions.

QUESTION: Are you ready to begin the process of character refinement?

Song: *Take Me into the Holy of Holies* by Paul Wilbur

The Menorah

The frequency associated with the Menorah is 528hz, the color is green/gold and it is associated with repairing DNA, initiating transformation and miracles.

Song: *Light of the World* by Lauren Daigle

Exodus 25:31-40 "Then you shall make a lampstand of pure gold. The lampstand *and* its base and its shaft are to be made of hammered work; its cups, its bulbs and its flowers shall be *of one piece* with it. Six branches shall go out from its sides; three branches of the lampstand from its one side and three branches of the lampstand from its other side. Three cups *shall be* shaped like almond *blossoms* in the one branch, a bulb and a flower, and three cups shaped like almond *blossoms* in the other branch, a bulb and a flower--so for six branches going out from the lampstand; and in the lampstand four cups shaped like almond *blossoms,* its bulbs and its flowers.

A bulb shall be under the *first* pair of branches *coming* out of it, and a bulb under the *second* pair of branches *coming* out of it, and a bulb under the *third* pair of branches *coming* out of it, for the six branches coming out of the lampstand. Their bulbs and their branches *shall be of one piece* with it; all of it shall be one piece of hammered work of pure gold. Then you shall make its lamps seven *in number;* and they shall mount its lamps so as to shed light on the space in front of it. Its snuffers and their trays *shall be* of pure gold. It shall be made from a talent of pure gold, with all these utensils. See that you make *them* after the pattern for them, which was shown to you on the mountain.

Psalm 119:105, Your word is a lamp to my feet and a light to my path.

The furniture in the courtyard of the Tabernacle is for cleansing us of darkness --- the sins, iniquities, transgressions that are in us, passed down from generation to generation since the beginning of time. The Holy Place of the Tabernacle is where our character is refined; where we overcome sin, iniquity, transgression through the Blood of the Lamb. Things made by man look beautiful and perfect until you put them under high-power magnification; it is then that you see the flaws and imperfections. Things created by YHVH are perfect and beautiful even when looked at under high-power magnification. The Lampstand was made of pure, hammered gold fashioned by an expert and gifted craftsman. We are like the lampstand, our beautiful raw material, or infant self was taken and fashioned into the person we are today by our parents, family, teachers, friends, and spiritual leaders. Most likely they weren't skilled and gifted craftsmen which resulted in flaws in our character development. Malachi 3:3 says that, "He [YHVH} will sit as a smelter and purifier of silver, and He will purify the sons of Levi and refine them like gold and silver, so that they may present to YHVH offerings in righteousness." A story is told of a lady that wanted a deeper understanding of this scripture so she went to a silversmith and asked him about the process of refining silver. After explaining to her about smelting to remove the impurities, temperature control and constant surveillance she thanked him and was about to take her leave when he called to her and asked her if she wanted to know the most important part of the process. She stopped, turned back to him and said, "There is more?" He replied, "It is when I see my face perfectly reflected in the silver that I know it is time to take the metal from the smelter.

YHVH allows us to be put in the smelter, or the 'furnace of affliction' for the refinement of our character. When our character is refined He shapes us into a vessel fit for His use. He pours the pure oil of His Spirit into us. The pure oil produces a flame that reflects off the pure, hammered gold of our character causing us to shine brightly thus illuminating a dark and dying world. Affliction produces character. YHVH will not keep you in the furnace one moment longer than is necessary for your refinement. To do so would cause your ruination. He wants you to be an overcomer of sin, iniquity and transgression, not just repent of these, but overcome them!

The seven branches of the Menorah represent the seven days of creation, the seven yearly feasts of YHVH, the seven spirits of YHVH as described in Isaiah 11, and the messages to the seven congregations described in the book of Revelation.

The First Branch of the seven-branched menorah represents the first day of creation, light and darkness; the first feast in the yearly feast cycle, Pesach or Passover; the congregation of Ephesus from Revelation 2:1-7; and the Spirit of Wisdom from Isaiah 11:2.

The congregation of Ephesus is commended for their perseverance and endurance, but chastised for having left their first love. To him who overcomes, Yashua said He would grant to eat of the Tree of Life which is in the Paradise of Elohe.

Revelation 2:1-7, "To the angel of the church in Ephesus write: The One who holds the seven stars in His right hand, the One who walks among the seven golden lampstands, says this: 'I know your deeds and your toil and perseverance, and that you cannot tolerate evil men, and you put to the test those who call themselves apostles, and they are not, and you found them to be false; and you have perseverance and have endured for My name's sake, and have not grown weary. 'But I have this against you, that you have left your first love. 'Therefore remember from where you have fallen, and repent and do the deeds you did at first; or else I am coming to you and will remove your lampstand out of its place--unless you repent. 'Yet this you do have, that you hate the deeds of the Nicolaitans, which I also hate. 'He who has an ear, let him hear what the Spirit says to the churches. To him who overcomes, I will grant to eat of the tree of life which is in the Paradise of God.'

> **Prayer:** Father YHVH in Heaven forgive me where I have sinned against You. Forgive me for when I have chosen to walk in darkness instead of light; forgive me when I have spurned Your Spirit of Wisdom and chosen to listen to the voice of folly instead. Forgive me for not humbling myself to remember my deliverance from bondage by way of Your sacrifice on Calvary's cross in the celebration of Pesach or Passover. Father YHVH I give to You the things which I have allowed to steal away the incredible first love and delight I once knew with You. Please remove from me the distractions that I

have allowed into my life that blind my vision of You. I desire to be an overcomer, I want to be an overcomer, I need to be an overcomer. Please hear my prayer and restore to me the joy of my Salvation.

The Second Branch of the seven-branched menorah represents the second day of creation, separating the waters; the second feast in the yearly feast cycle, Unleavened Bread; the congregation of Smyrna from Revelation 2:8-11; and the Spirit of Understanding from Isaiah 11:2.

The congregation of Smyrna is commended by Yashua for remaining steadfast in spite of persecution, tribulation and poverty; they are one of two congregations that are not chastised, but encouraged to continue to persevere and receive a crown of life.

Revelation 2:8-11, "And to the angel of the church in Smyrna write: The first and the last, who was dead, and has come to life, says this: 'I know your tribulation and your poverty (but you are rich), and the blasphemy by those who say they are Jews and are not, but are a synagogue of Satan. 'Do not fear what you are about to suffer. Behold, the devil is about to cast some of you into prison, so that you will be tested, and you will have tribulation for ten days. Be faithful until death, and I will give you the crown of life. 'He who has an ear, let him hear what the Spirit says to the churches. He who overcomes will not be hurt by the second death.'

> **Prayer:** Father, sometimes I confess that it is difficult to stand in the face of tribulation; it is difficult to endure poverty, it seems like my life is one test after another. Please forgive me when I complain, when I forget that in You I am rich, in You I have my hope, my strength, my life. Forgive me when I take my eyes off You and falter on my way. Thank you, that when I cry out to You --- You are there to lift me back into the safety of Your arms. Help me to overcome the snares of the evil one, help me to be faithful unto death.

The Third Branch of the seven-branched menorah represents the third day of creation, Earth, fruit, seed and plants; the third feast in the yearly feast cycle, First Fruits of Barley harvest; the congregation of Perganum from Revelation 2:12-17; and the Spirit of Counsel from Isaiah 11:2.

The congregation of Perganum is commended by Yashua for holding fast to My Name and not denying My faith, but chastised for allowing false teaching and immorality among the brethren. Those who overcome will be given some of the hidden manna, and a white stone and a new name written on the stone.

Revelation 2:12-17, "And to the angel of the church in

Pergamum write: The One who has the sharp two-edged sword says this: 'I know where you dwell, where Satan's throne is; and you hold fast My name, and did not deny My faith even in the days of Antipas, My witness, My faithful one, who was killed among you, where Satan dwells. 'But I have a few things against you, because you have there some who hold the teaching of Balaam, who kept teaching Balak to put a stumbling block before the sons of Israel, to eat things sacrificed to idols and to commit acts of immorality. 'So you also have some who in the same way hold the teaching of the Nicolaitans. 'Therefore repent; or else I am coming to you quickly, and I will make war against them with the sword of My mouth. 'He who has an ear, let him hear what the Spirit says to the churches. To him who overcomes, to him I will give some of the hidden manna, and I will give him a white stone, and a new name written on the stone which no one knows but he who receives it.'

> **Prayer:** Heavenly Father, I want my life to reflect good soil that produces thirty, sixty, a hundred fold increase to the glory of Your Name and kingdom. Please, may the words that I speak be Your Words; may my life reflect Your Spirit of Counsel. May I daily eat from the Bread of Life that gives eternal life. Help me to remember that it is only as I come to You do I have life. Let the things of this world grow dim and fade away in the light of Your glorious grace.

The Fourth Branch of the seven-branched menorah represents the fourth day of creation, the sun, moon and the stars; the fourth feast in the yearly feast cycle, Shavu'ot or Pentecost; the congregation of Thyatira from Revelation 2:18-29; and the Spirit of Adonai from Isaiah 11:2.

The congregation of Thyatira is commended for their love and faith and service and perseverance and great deeds, but they are chastised for tolerating the spirit of Jezebel who leads My bondservants astray... He who overcomes and keeps My deeds until the end, to him I will give authority over the nations... as I also have received authority from My Father.

Revelation 2:18-29, "And to the angel of the church in Thyatira write: The Son of God, who has eyes like a flame of fire, and His feet are like burnished bronze, says this: 'I know your deeds, and your love and faith and service and perseverance, and that your deeds of late are greater than at first. 'But I have this against you, that you tolerate the woman Jezebel, who calls herself a prophetess, and she teaches and leads My bond-servants astray so that they commit acts of immorality and eat things sacrificed to idols. 'I gave her time to repent, and she does not want to repent of her immorality. 'Behold, I will throw her on a bed of sickness, and those who commit adultery with her into great tribulation, unless they repent of her deeds. 'And I will kill her children with pestilence, and all the churches will know that I am He who searches the minds and hearts; and I will give to each one of you according to your deeds. 'But I say to you, the rest who are in Thyatira, who do not hold this teaching, who have not known the deep things of Satan, as they call them--I place no other burden on you. 'Nevertheless what you have, hold fast until I come. 'He who overcomes, and he who keeps My deeds until the end, TO HIM I WILL GIVE AUTHORITY OVER THE NATIONS; AND HE SHALL RULE THEM WITH A ROD OF IRON, AS THE VESSELS OF THE POTTER ARE BROKEN TO PIECES, as I also have received authority from My Father; and I will give him the morning star. 'He who has an ear, let him hear what the Spirit says to the churches.'

> **Prayer:** Abba, my Father, fill me anew with Your Holy Spirit. And please forgive me for looking to myself to satisfy my desires, and wants. Forgive me for tolerating things that I should take a firm stand against. Oh Father in Heaven I want to be holy as You are holy, I want to be Your pure and spotless bride. Help me to run my race through to the end that I not falter or faint. Whatever would seek to hinder me please help me to lay aside every burden and the sin which so easily entangles me, and let me run with endurance the race that is set before me. Help me to fix my eyes on Yashua, the author and perfecter of faith, who for the joy set before Him endured the cross, despising the shame, and has sat down

at the right hand of the throne of YHVH.

The Fifth Branch of the seven-branched menorah represents the fifth day of creation, the birds and the fish; the fifth feast in the yearly feast cycle, Yom Teruah or Trumpets; the congregation of Sardis from Revelation 3:1-6; and the Spirit of Power from Isaiah 11:2.

The congregation of Sardis is not commended by Yashua for any worthy deeds, but rather are chastised; wake-up and strengthen the things that remain, which are about to die, for I have not found your deeds complete in the sight of YHVH. Remember what you have seen and heard and keep it and repent. He who overcomes shall be clothed in white garments; and I will not erase his name from the book of life.

Revelation 3:1-6, "To the angel of the church in Sardis write: He who has the seven Spirits of God and the seven stars, says this: 'I know your deeds, that you have a name that you are alive, but you are dead. Wake up, and strengthen the things that remain, which were about to die; for I have not found your deeds completed in the sight of My God. So remember what you have received and heard; and keep it, and repent. Therefore if you do not wake up, I will come like a thief, and you will not know at what hour I will come to you. But you have a few people in Sardis who have not soiled their garments; and they will walk with Me in white, for they are worthy. He who overcomes will thus be clothed in white garments; and I will not erase his name from the book of life, and I will confess his name before My Father and before His angels. He who has an ear, let him hear what the Spirit says to the churches.'"

> **Prayer:** My Father in Heaven, I have been asleep. Forgive me for being foolish and allowing my light to go out. I recognize that I have let satan steal from me; and I know that I must and I willingly do take responsibility for allowing this thievery by the enemy of the brethren. I repent for my lack of alertness and steadfastness to stand on Your Word. I renounce hasatan's schemes and devices he uses against me and I ask that his controlling, manipulating, presence be removed from manifesting in my life. I resist his worldly influence in my life, I chose to submit my thoughts to You, YHVH, and resist the devil and he must flee from me. I rejoice that You are my Strength, my Deliverer, my Redeemer, my Provider, my Healer; that You are All Present, All Knowing and All Powerful. Thank you for restoring to me the joy of my Salvation!

The Sixth Branch of the seven-branched menorah represents the sixth day of creation, man and beasts; the sixth feast in the yearly feast cycle, Yom Kippur of the Day of Atonement; the congregation of Philadelphia from Revelation 3:7-13; and the Spirit of Knowledge from Isaiah 11:2.

The congregation of Philadelphia is commended for keeping My word and having not denied My Name; they are encouraged to hold fast what you have in order that no one take your crown. He who overcomes I will make him a pillar in the temple of My Elohe and he will not go out from it anymore.

Revelation 3:7-13, "And to the angel of the church in Philadelphia write: He who is holy, who is true, who has the key of David, who opens and no one will shut, and who shuts and no one opens, says this: I know your deeds. Behold, I have put before you an open door which no one can shut, because you have a little power, and have kept My word, and have not denied My name. Behold, I will cause those of the synagogue of Satan, who say that they are Jews and are not, but lie--I will make them come and bow down at your feet, and make them know that I have loved you. Because you have kept the word of My perseverance, I also will keep you from the hour of testing, that hour which is about to come upon the whole world, to test those who dwell on the earth. I am coming quickly; hold fast what you have, so that no one will take your crown. He who overcomes, I will make him a pillar in the temple of My God, and he will not go out from it anymore; and I will write on him the name of My God, and the name of the city of My God, the new Jerusalem, which comes down out of heaven from My God, and My new name. He who has an ear, let him hear what the Spirit says to the churches."

Prayer: Father, thank you that Your Words are Yes and Amen; thank you that You are the way, the truth and the life. Thank you that there is no shadow of turning with You. Thank you that nothing is impossible for You. Thank you for holding me in the palm of Your hand where the enemy of the brethren cannot snatch me away. I love You Abba --- thank you for loving me first so I can love You! Thank you, Yashua, for giving up Your life on Calvary's tree that I might have life with You for all eternity. Thank you that it is through Your power that I can overcome. Open my ears, Abba, that I might hear all that You say to me. Forgive me for the times when I didn't respond to Your voice.

The Seventh Branch of the seven-branched menorah represents the seventh day of creation, the Shabbat; the seventh feast in the yearly feast cycle, Sukkot or Tabernacles; the congregation of Laodicea from Revelation 3:14-22; and the Spirit of Reverence from Isaiah 11:2.

The congregation of Laodicea was not commended by Yashua for any worthy acts, but rather strongly chastised for their luke-warm behavior; I would that you were hot or cold, but because you are neither hot or cold I will spit

you out of My mouth. But Yashua does say to the congregation of Laodicea --- those whom I love, I reprove and discipline, be zealous therefore and repent. He who overcomes I will grant to him to sit down with Me on My throne.

Revelation 3:14-22, "To the angel of the church in Laodicea write: The Amen, the faithful and true Witness, the Beginning of the creation of God, says this: I know your deeds, that you are neither cold nor hot; I wish that you were cold or hot. So because you are lukewarm, and neither hot nor cold, I will spit you out of My mouth. Because you say, "I am rich, and have become wealthy, and have need of nothing," and you do not know that you are wretched and miserable and poor and blind and naked, I advise you to buy from Me gold refined by fire so that you may become rich, and white garments so that you may clothe yourself, and that the shame of your nakedness will not be revealed; and eye salve to anoint your eyes so that you may see. Those whom I love, I reprove and discipline; therefore be zealous and repent. Behold, I stand at the door and knock; if anyone hears My voice and opens the door, I will come in to him and will dine with him, and he with Me. He who overcomes, I will grant to him to sit down with Me on My throne, as I also overcame and sat down with My Father on His throne. He who has an ear, let him hear what the Spirit says to the churches."

Prayer: My Father in Heaven, I have sinned against You by not honoring You on the day You set apart for my benefit. I have dishonored You by thinking I can do this thing called "life" without Your help. I think I am okay, but from Your Eyes I am in miserable circumstances. My choices and decisions are putting me at risk of being excluded from Your Kingdom. Oh Father, I am so like the Emperor who was deceived into thinking he was wearing the most elegant of clothes when actually he was naked. Oh Abba, forgive me for my arrogance, my rebellion, idolatry and pride. I confess, I am guilty of fault-finding, harboring a harsh spirit, superficiality, defensiveness, lack of humility, presumption, desperation for attention, and neglecting others that seem to serve me no useful end. Refine me, please, do whatever it may take to restore me to Your favor. Come into my heart and clean my house, I pray.

The Table of Showbread

The frequency associated with the Table of Showbread is 639hz, the color is forest green and it is associated with enabling connections and relationships.

Song: *Bread of Heaven* by Silvana Martins and Jeremy Lee Johnson

Exodus 25:23-30 "You shall make a table of acacia wood, two cubits long and one cubit wide and one and a half cubits high. You shall overlay it with pure gold and make a gold border around it. You shall make for it a rim of a handbreadth around *it;* and you shall make a gold border for the rim around it. You shall make four gold rings for it and put rings on the four corners which are on its four feet. The rings shall be close to the rim as holders for the poles to carry the table. You shall make the poles of acacia wood and overlay them with gold, so that with them the table may be carried. You shall make its dishes and its pans and its jars and its bowls with which to pour drink offerings; you shall make them of pure gold. You shall set the bread of the Presence on the table before Me at all times.

*The Bread of the Presence symbolizes complete dependence on YHVH Yashua for our every need. Yashua said in **Matthew 6:31-34** "Do not worry then, saying, 'What will we eat?' or 'What will we drink?' or 'What will we wear for clothing?' For the Gentiles eagerly seek all these things; for your heavenly Father knows that you need all these things. **"But seek first His kingdom and His righteousness, and all these things will be added to you.** So do not worry about tomorrow; for tomorrow will care for itself. Each day has enough trouble of its own."*

Every week the Priest put 12 fresh unleavened breads on the Table of the Bread of the Presence. These twelve loaves represent the 12 tribes of Israel. As believers in Yashua we are part of these tribes of Israel. As part of the tribes of Israel we have a guarantee from YHVH Yashua that He will never leave us or forsake us! (Deu 31:8 and Heb 13:5-6) We are to look to Him for our every need.

Reuben, for she said, "Because YHVH has seen my **affliction…**

She conceived again, **Simeon,** "Because YHVH has heard that I am **unloved**...

She conceived again **Levi,** "Now this time my husband will become **attached** to me... (or will cease from rejecting me).

She named him **Judah.** "This time I will **praise** YHVH**."**

Rachel said, **Dan,** "God has **vindicated** me.

Rachel said, **Naphtali,** "With mighty **wrestlings** I have wrestled...

Leah said, "How **fortunate**!" So she named him **Gad**.

Leah said, **Asher, "Happy** am I!

Leah said, **Issachar,** "God has given me my **wages**...

Leah said, **Zebulun,** "God has endowed me with **a good gift...**

Rachel conceived **Joseph,** "God has taken away my **reproach."**

Rachel began to give birth she named him Ben-oni; but his father called him **Benjamin**. [**son of my right hand**]

Are you afflicted, unloved, rejected; are you praising, vindicated, wrestling; are you fortunate, happy, well-paid; are you endowed with good gifts, have you suffered reproach; are you a child of the right-hand? If any of these reflect you --- then you are a part of one of the tribes as a believer and partaker of Yashua's free gift of Salvation. Eat freely from the table He has prepared for you!

John 6:33 "For the bread of God is that which comes down out of heaven, and gives life to the world."

John 6:35 Yashua said to them, "I am the bread of life; he who comes to Me will not hunger, and he who believes in Me will never thirst.

John 6:47-48 "Truly, truly, I say to you, he who believes has eternal life. "I am the bread of life.

John 6:51-58 "I am the living bread that came down out of heaven; if anyone eats of this bread, he will live forever; and the bread also which I will give for the life of the world is My flesh."

Then the Jews *began* to argue with one another, saying, "How can this man give us *His* flesh to eat?"

So Yashua said to them, "Truly, truly, I say to you, unless you eat the flesh of the Son of Man and drink His blood, you have no life in yourselves. He who eats My flesh and drinks My blood has eternal life, and I will raise him up on the last day. For My flesh is true food, and My blood is true drink. He who eats My flesh and drinks My blood abides in Me, and I in him. As the living Father sent Me, and I live because of the Father, so he who eats Me, he also will live because of Me. This is the bread which came down out of heaven; not as the fathers ate and died; he who eats this bread will live forever."

John 4:31-34, Meanwhile the disciples were urging Him, saying, "Rabbi, eat." But He said to them, "I have food to eat that you do not know about. "So the disciples were saying to one another, "No one brought Him *anything* to eat, did he?" Yashua said to them, "My food is to do the will of Him who sent Me and to accomplish His work."

John 6:26-29, Yashua answered them and said, "Truly, truly, I say to you, you seek Me, not because you saw signs, but because you ate of the loaves and were filled. "Do not work for the food which perishes, but for the food which endures to eternal life, which the Son of Man will give to you, for on Him the Father, God, has set His seal." Therefore they said to Him, "What shall we do, so that we may work the works of God?" Yashua answered and said to them, "This is the work of God that you believe in Him whom He has sent."

Exodus 34:27-28, Then YHVH said to Moses, "Write down these words, for in accordance with these words I have made a covenant with you and with Israel." So he was there with YHVH forty days and forty nights; he did not eat bread or drink water. And he wrote on the tablets the words of the covenant, the Ten Commandments.

1Kings 19:5-8, He lay down and slept under a juniper tree; and behold, there was an angel touching him, and he said to him, "Arise, eat. "Then he looked and behold, there was at his head a bread cake *baked on* hot stones, and a jar of water. So he ate and drank and lay down again. The angel of YHVH came again a second time and touched him and said, "Arise, eat, because the journey is too great for you. "So he arose and ate and drank, and went in the strength of that food forty days and forty nights to Horeb, the mountain of God.

Proverbs 23:1-8 When you sit down to dine with a ruler, consider carefully what is before you, and put a knife to your throat If you are a man of appetite. Do not desire his delicacies, for it is deceptive food. Do not weary yourself to gain wealth, cease from your consideration *of it.* When you set your eyes on it, it is gone; for *wealth* certainly makes itself wings like an eagle that flies *toward* the heavens. Do not eat the bread of a selfish man, or desire his delicacies; for as he thinks within himself, so he is. He says to you, "Eat and drink!" But his heart is not with you. You will vomit up the morsel you have eaten, and waste your compliments.

Are you looking to the hand of Yashua to take care of your physical needs --- or do you believe that He will take care of you – period, no matter what --- eternally?

Psalm 23 A Psalm of David. YHVH is my shepherd, I shall not want. He makes me lie down in green pastures; He leads me beside quiet waters. He restores my soul; He guides me in the paths of righteousness for His name's sake. Even though I walk through the valley of the shadow of death, I fear no evil, for You are with me; Your rod and Your staff, they comfort me. You prepare a table before me in the presence of my enemies; You have anointed my head with oil; my cup overflows. Surely goodness and lovingkindness will follow me all the days of my life, and I will dwell in the house of YHVH forever.

> **Prayer:** Father, I confess that I am guilty of relying on my own resources to take care of my needs. I have complained and grumbled at what I perceived as lack from Your hand. I have blamed You for my troubles when I chose to eat from the table of the world and not partake in the simple fare You have provided for me. I am guilty of seeking Your Hand (provision) above Your Face (relationship). I realize that when I rely on my own abilities I am guilty of vanity and pride. Forgive me, Abba, for not trusting You to sustain me through the struggles, trials and challenges of this earthly life. Yashua said in Matthew 16:24-26, "If anyone wishes to come after Me, he must deny himself, and take up his cross and follow Me. For whoever wishes to save his life will lose it; but whoever loses his life for My sake will find it. For what will it profit a man if he gains the whole world and forfeits his soul?

Or what will a man give in exchange for his soul?" Help me Abba, to give up my right to myself for Your sake for I know that the only things that truly sustain and satisfy are You and You alone.

Deuteronomy 8:2-3, "You shall remember all the way which YHVH your God has led you in the wilderness these forty years, that He might humble you, testing you, to know what was in your heart, whether you would keep His commandments or not. He humbled you and let you be hungry, and fed you with manna which you did not know, nor did your fathers know, **that He might make you understand that man does not live by bread alone, but man lives by everything that proceeds out of the mouth of YHVH.**

The Incense Altar

The frequency associated with the Incense Altar is 741hz, the color is blue and it is associated with awakening your intuition.

Song: *I Am He* by Terry Talbot

Exodus 30:1-10 "Moreover, you shall make an altar as a place for burning incense; you shall make it of acacia wood. Its length *shall be* a cubit, and its width a cubit, it shall be square, and its height *shall be* two cubits; its horns *shall be* of one piece with it.

You shall overlay it with pure gold, its top and its sides all around, and its horns; and you shall make a gold molding all around for it. You shall make two gold rings for it under its molding; you shall make *them* on its two side walls--on opposite sides--and they shall be holders for poles with which to carry it. You shall make the poles of acacia wood and overlay them with gold. You shall put this altar in front of the veil that is near the ark of the testimony, in front of the mercy seat that is over *the ark of* the testimony, where I will meet with you. Aaron shall burn fragrant incense on it; he shall burn it every morning when he trims the lamps. When Aaron trims the lamps at twilight, he shall burn incense. *There shall be* perpetual incense before YHVH throughout your generations. You shall not offer any strange incense on this altar, or burnt offering or meal offering; and you shall not pour out a drink offering on it. Aaron shall make atonement on its horns once a year; he shall make atonement on it with the blood of the sin offering of atonement once a year throughout your generations. It is most holy to YHVH."

Hebrews 5:1-7 For every high priest taken from among men is appointed on behalf of men in things pertaining to God, in order to offer both gifts and sacrifices for sins; he can deal gently with the ignorant and misguided, since he himself also is beset with weakness; and because of it he is obligated to offer sacrifices for sins, as for the people, so also for himself. And no one takes the honor to himself, but receives it when he is called by God, even as Aaron was. So also Yashua did not glorify Himself so as to become a high priest, but He who said to Him, "YOU ARE MY SON, TODAY I HAVE BEGOTTEN YOU"; just as He says also in another passage, "YOU ARE A PRIEST FOREVER ACCORDING TO THE ORDER OF MELCHIZEDEK." In the days of His flesh, He offered up both prayers and supplications with loud crying and tears to the One able to save Him from death, and He was heard because of His piety.

There are two aspects of Melchizedek: 1st as King of Righteousness, 2nd as King of Peace. Righteousness is to make things right with or be justified before YHVH. We have to make things right between ourselves and YHVH to be at peace with YHVH. We cannot have peace, true peace, if we at odds with YHVH.

In the courtyard of the Tabernacle before the Brazen Altar and the Laver you have confessed your sins, iniquities and transgressions; holding fast to the promise that if we confess our sins He who is faithful will forgive us our sins, iniquities and transgressions and cleanse us of all unrighteousness. At the Menorah and the Table of Showbread you have learned how to overcome sin, iniquity and transgression by casting all your cares on Yashua who cares for you and by seeking first the kingdom of YHVH and His righteousness; now, here at the Altar of Incense you stand and present your case for His righteous judgment.

Our prayers before YHVH ascend as fragrant incense when they are devoid of fear and full of faith. Faith is doing what you have been commissioned to do; to be holy as He is holy or to take a firm stand against evil. For six thousand years evil has been multiplying upon evil; transgression upon transgression, iniquity upon iniquity;

none of us are righteous no not one, but our Advocate is righteous and He told us to cast all of our cares upon Him.

What is the will of YHVH?

That we be holy as He is holy!

So whatever sin, iniquity, and transgression that you have laid on the altar and washed away in the laver; whatever character refinement YHVH has perfected in your life, now is the time to present the facts of your case before the Throne of grace and ask for a just judgment of mercy. That is, His heart; mercy triumphing over judgment, (James 2:13). It is here that we now offer prayers that reflect the heart of YHVH --- a heart of peace and righteousness.

Hebrews 4:12-16 For the word of God is living and active and sharper than any two-edged sword, and piercing as far as the division of soul and spirit, of both joints and marrow, and able to judge the thoughts and intentions of the heart. And there is no creature hidden from His sight, but all things are open and laid bare to the eyes of Him with whom we have to do. Therefore, since we have a great high priest who has passed through the heavens, Yashua the Son of YHVH, let us hold fast our confession. For we do not have a high priest who cannot sympathize with our weaknesses, but One who has been tempted in all things as we are, yet without sin. Therefore let us draw near with confidence to the throne of grace, so that we may receive mercy and find grace to help in time of need.

> **Prayer:** "Abba, I know that I am a product of a sinful bloodline. I see pride and rebellion and idolatry manifesting it's ugly head in so many areas of my life; _____. I can also see that I have inherited generational iniquities and transgressions, _____. I am guilty of partaking in these things that are offensive abominations to You, but at your gentle guidance I have laid myself on Your Altar, I have washed myself at Your Laver, I have stood before Your Light and I have eaten from Your Table. I now stand before Your Incense Altar and ask for Your Mercy to judge me and my bloodline with justice for You are The Righteous Judge. I humbly ask that these sins, iniquities, and transgressions that I have laid before You be wiped out of my book so that I might be pure and clean before you; that the adversary of the brethren have no more occasion to accuse me or my bloodline of these things. I thank you for Your mercy, Your loving kindness, and Your compassion that fails not.

We have come to this altar empty of self, but full to over-flowing of the love and mercy and grace of our beloved Bridegroom, Yashua. It is truly the Father's heart that we want to hear as we prepare to come to Him and lean our head upon His breast.

And so we wait to hear His judgment concerning whatever situation we may be presenting to Him.

Revelation 5:8-10, When He had taken the book, the four living creatures and the twenty-four elders fell down before the Lamb, each one holding a harp and golden bowls full of incense, which are the prayers of the saints. And they sang a new song, saying, "Worthy are You to take the book and to break its seals; for You were slain, and purchased for God with Your blood men from every tribe and tongue and people and nation. You have made them to be a kingdom and priests to our God; and they will reign upon the earth."

Revelation 8:3-4, Another angel came and stood at the altar, holding a golden censer; and much incense was given to him, so that he might add it to the prayers of all the saints on the golden altar which was before the throne. And the smoke of the incense, with the prayers of the saints, went up before God out of the angel's hand.

> **Our Father** who art in Heaven, hallowed be Thy Name. Thy kingdom come, Thy will be done on earth as it is in heaven. Give us this day our daily bread and forgive us our sins as we forgive those
>
> who sin against us. Lead us not into temptation, but deliver us from evil; for Thine is the kingdom and the power and the glory, forever. AMEN

The Third Veil --- "Hallelujah! For YHVH our God, the Almighty, reigns. Let us rejoice and be glad and give the glory to Him, for the marriage of the Lamb has come and His bride has made herself ready. It was given to her to clothe herself in fine linen, bright and clean; for the fine linen is the righteous acts of the saints."

QUESTION: Are you ready to meet with the Great King?

He is waiting for you!

Song: *We Fall Down* by Chris Tomlin

The Ark of the Covenant

The frequency associated with the Ark of the Covenant is 852hz, the color is purple and it is associated with helping you return to spiritual order.

Song: *The Great I Am* by New Life Worship

Exodus 25:10-22 "They shall construct an ark of acacia wood two and a half cubits long, and one and a half cubits wide, and one and a half cubits high. You shall overlay it with pure gold, inside and out you shall overlay it, and you shall make a gold molding around it. You shall cast four gold rings for it and fasten them on its four feet, and two rings shall be on one side of it and two rings on the other side of it. You shall make poles of acacia wood and overlay them with gold. You shall put the poles into the rings on the sides of the ark, to carry the ark with them. The poles shall remain in the rings of the ark; they shall not be removed from it. You shall put into the ark the testimony which I shall give you. You shall make a mercy seat of pure gold, two and a half cubits long and one and a half cubits wide. You shall make two cherubim of gold, make them of hammered work at the two ends of the mercy seat. Make one cherub at one end and one cherub at the other end; you shall make the cherubim *of one piece* with the mercy seat at its two ends. The cherubim shall have *their* wings spread upward, covering the mercy seat with their wings and facing one another; the faces of the cherubim are to be *turned* toward the mercy seat. You shall put the mercy seat on top of the ark, and in the ark you shall put the testimony which I will give to you. There I will meet with you; and from above the mercy seat, from between the two cherubim which are upon the ark of the testimony; I will speak to you about all that I will give you in commandment for the sons of Israel.

Deuteronomy 10:1-5, "At that time YHVH said to me, 'Cut out for yourself two tablets of stone like the former ones, and come up to Me on the mountain, and make an ark of wood for yourself. 'I will write on the tablets the words that were on the former tablets which you shattered, and you shall put them in the ark.' So I made an ark of acacia wood and cut out two tablets of stone like the former ones, and went up on the mountain with the two tablets in my hand. He wrote on the tablets, like the former writing, the Ten Commandments which YHVH had spoken to you on the mountain from the midst of

the fire on the day of the assembly; and YHVH gave them to me. Then I turned and came down from the mountain and put the tablets in the ark which I had made; and there they are, as YHVH commanded me."

YHVH, for the second time, wrote His commandments on two new tablets of stone; indicating how He would rewrite His law on the human heart through Messiah Yashua.

Jeremiah 31:31, 33, "Behold, days are coming," declares YHVH, "when I will make a new covenant with the house of Israel and with the house of Judah... But this is the covenant which I will make with the house of Israel after those days," declares YHVH, "I will put My law within them and on their heart I will write it; and I will be their God, and they shall be My people."

YHVH's laws are eternal; the words He wrote on the second set of tablets were identical to His words on the first set, pointing to the fact that YHVH does not change; He is the same yesterday, today and forever.

Psalm 9:7-8 But YHVH abides forever; He has established His throne for judgment, and He will judge the world in righteousness; He will execute judgment for the peoples with equity.

1Timothy 6:13-16 I charge you in the presence of God, who gives life to all things, and of Messiah Yashua, who testified the good confession before Pontius Pilate, that you keep the commandment without stain or reproach until the appearing of our Adonai Yashua haMashiach, which He will bring about at the proper time--He who is the blessed and only Sovereign, the King of kings and Lord of lords, who alone possesses immortality and dwells in unapproachable light, whom no man has seen or can see. To Him be honor and eternal dominion! Amen.

Revelation 17:14 "These will wage war against the Lamb, and the Lamb will overcome them, because He is Lord of lords and King of kings, and those who are with Him are the called and chosen and faithful."

Revelation 19:7-16 "Let us rejoice and be glad and give the glory to Him, for the marriage of the Lamb has come and His bride has made herself ready." It was given to her to clothe herself in fine linen, bright and clean; for the fine linen is the righteous acts of the saints. Then he said to me, "Write, 'Blessed are those who are invited to the marriage supper of the Lamb.'" And he *said to me, "These are true words of God." Then I fell at his feet to worship him. But he said to me, "Do not do that; I am a fellow servant of yours and your brethren who hold the testimony of Yashua; worship God. For the testimony of Yashua is the spirit of prophecy." And I saw heaven opened, and behold, a white horse, and He who sat on it is called Faithful and True, and in righteousness He judges and wages war. His eyes are a flame of fire, and on His head are many diadems; and He has a name written on Him which no one knows except Himself. He is clothed with a robe dipped in blood, and His name is called The Word of God. And the armies which are in heaven, clothed in fine linen, white and clean, were following Him on white horses. From His mouth comes a sharp sword, so that with it He may strike down the nations, and He will rule them with a rod of iron; and He treads the wine press of the fierce wrath of God, the Almighty. And on His robe and on His thigh He has a name written, "KING OF KINGS, AND LORD OF LORDS."

Through Messiah Yashua mankind is restored in relationship to His Creator. He is trustworthy to render righteous judgment. Hear and obey; Shema, Israel!

> **Prayer:** Almighty YHVH, Creator of heaven and earth I bow before you and with great reverence and humility say, "Thank you! Thank you, for restoring me in right relationship to you!"

Revelation 7:9-16, After these things I looked, and behold, a great multitude which no one could count, from every nation and all tribes and peoples and tongues, standing before the throne and before the Lamb, clothed in white robes, and palm branches were in their hands; and they cry out with a loud voice, saying, "Salvation to our God who sits on the throne, and to the

Lamb." And all the angels were standing around the throne and around the elders and the four living creatures; and they fell on their faces before the throne and worshiped God, saying, "Amen, blessing and glory and wisdom and thanksgiving and honor and power and might, be to our God forever and ever. Amen." Then one of the elders answered, saying to me, "These who are clothed in the white robes, who are they, and where have they come from?" I said to him, "My lord, you know." And he said to me, "These are the ones who come out of the great tribulation, and they have washed their robes and made them white in the blood of the Lamb. For this reason, they are before the throne of God; and they serve Him day and night in His temple; and He who sits on the throne will spread His tabernacle over them. They will hunger no longer, nor thirst anymore; nor will the sun beat down on them, nor any heat; for the Lamb in the center of the throne will be their shepherd, and will guide them to springs of the water of life; and God will wipe every tear from their eyes."

Even so come Adonai, Yashua!

Take time to rest in this holy place --- do not leave YHVH's presence while the anointing oil is still upon you! (Lev 10:7)

Made in the USA
Charleston, SC
14 October 2015